HOW TO MANAGE STRESS PROPERLY: Turning stress into a better life.

Sylvester B. Scott

Table of contents

Chapter 1

Stress affects us all. You may notice symptoms of stress when chastising your kiddies, during busy times at work, when managing your finances, or when managing a grueling relationship. Stress is far and wide. And while a little stress is OK! Some stress is actually salutary, too important stress can wear you down and make you sick, both mentally and physically.

The first step to controlling stress is to know the symptoms of stress. But feting stress symptoms may be harder than you suppose. The utmost of us are so habituated to being stressed, we frequently do not know we're stressed until we're at the breaking point.

What Is Stress?

Stress is the body's response to dangerous situations, whether they're real or perceived. When you feel hovered, a chemical response occurs in your body that allows you to act in a way to help injury. This response is known as "fight- or- flight" or the stress response. During the stress response, your heart rate increases, breathing quickens, muscles strain, and blood pressure rises. You 've gotten ready to act. It's how you cover yourself.

Stress means different effects to different people. What causes stress in one person may be of little concern to another. Some people are more suitable to handle stress than others. And, not all stress is bad. In small boluses, stress can help you negotiate tasks and help you from getting hurt. For illustration, stress is what gets you to slam on the thickets to avoid hitting the auto in front of you. That is a good thing. Our bodies are designed to handle small boluses of stress. But, we aren't equipped to handle long-term, habitual stress without ill consequences.

What Are the Symptoms of Stress?

Stress can affect all corridors of your life, including your feelings, actions, allowing capability, and physical health. No part of the body is vulnerable. But, because people handle stress differently, symptoms of stress can vary. Symptoms can be vague and may be the same as those caused by medical conditions. So it's important to bandy them with your croaker.

You may have any of the following symptoms of stress.

Emotional symptoms of stress include:

- Getting fluently agitated, frustrated, and temperamental
- Feeling overwhelmed, as if you're losing control or need to take control
- Having a hard time relaxing and quieting your mind
- Feeling bad about yourself (low tone- regard), and feeling lonely, empty, and depressed
- Avoiding others

Physical symptoms of stress include

- Low energy

- Headaches
- Upset stomach, including diarrhea, constipation, and nausea
- pangs, pains, and tense muscles
- casket pain and rapid-fire twinkle
- wakefulness
- Frequent snap and infections
- Loss of sexual desire and/or capability
- unease and shaking, ringing in the cognizance, and cold or sweaty hands and bases
- Dry mouth and a hard time swallowing
- Clenched jaw and grinding teeth

Cognitive symptoms of stress include:

- Constant fussing
- contendaching studies

- obliviousness and disorganization
- incapability to concentrate
- Poor judgment
- Being pessimistic or seeing only the negative side

Behavioral symptoms of stress include:

- Changes in appetite, either not eating or eating too important
- Procrastinating and avoiding liabilities
- further use of alcohol, medicines, or cigarettes
- Having further nervous actions, similar as nail smelling, wriggling, and pacing.

What Are the Consequences of Long-Term Stress?

A little stress every now and then isn't a commodity to be concerned about. But ongoing, habitual stress can beget or worsen numerous serious health problems, including;

- Mental health problems, similar as depression, anxiety, and personality diseases
- Cardiovascular complaint, including heart complaint, high blood pressure, abnormal heart measures, heart attacks, and strokes
- Rotundity and other eating diseases
- Menstrual problems
- Sexual dysfunction, similar as incompetence and unseasonable interjection in men and loss of sexual desire in men and women

- Skin and hair problems, similar as acne, psoriasis, and eczema, and endless hair loss
- Gastrointestinal problems, similar as GERD, gastritis, ulcerative colitis, and perverse colon

Help Is Available for Stress

Stress is a part of life. What matters most is how you handle it. The stylish thing you can do to help stress load and the health consequences that come with it's to know your stress symptoms. Still, talk to croaker.

If you or a loved one is feeling overwhelmed by stress. numerous symptoms of stress can also be signs of other health problems. Your croaker can estimate your symptoms and rule

out other conditions. However, your croaker
can recommend a therapist or counselor to help you better handle your stress, If stress is to condemn.

The Causes of Stress

Stress is different for everyone. What stresses you out may not indeed bother your stylish friend and vice versa. But numerous causes of stress can have a negative impact, including;

- Being bullied
- Working too hard
- Losing a job
- Marriage or relationship problems
- Recent break up or disjoin
- Death in the family
- Difficulty in academy
- Family problems
- Busy schedule
- Recent move

Still, our bodies reply the same to stressors. That's because the response is your body's way of dealing with tough or demanding situations. It causes hormonal, respiratory, cardiovascular, and nervous system changes. For illustration, stress can make your heart beat briskly, make you breathe fleetly, sweat, and tense up. It can also give you a burst of energy.

This is known as the body's "fight- or- flight response." It's this chemical response that prepares your body for a physical response because it thinks it's under attack. This type of stress helped our mortal ancestors survive in nature.

Stress opinion

Still, it's a good idea to talk with a specialist who can help. If you're having trouble managing stress or your response to a certain event is more violent and lasts longer than usual.

They'll presumably ask you some questions related to the following;

- Whether a traumatic life event happened within the once 3 months
- Whether your stress situations are advanced than usual when you reply to situations at home or at work
- If your stress might be related to grieving
- If you have a internal complaint that might be linked to your stress
- Grounded on your answers to these questions and other areas you talk about, the specialist can recommend some effects that can help.

Stress doesn't have to negatively affect you if you learn to handle it. A many effects you can try include;

- Fete what causes you stress at home or at work, and find ways to steer clear of those situations.
- Try not to take on too important and prioritize your pretensions. Cut yourself a break and be more forgiving when you don't get to everything.
- Being tone-critical can add to your stress. Replace negative studies with positive bones.
- Tell yourself "I suppose I can" rather than "I know I can't." produce a network of close musketeers and co-workers you can go to when stress starts to make. A hobby horse or a cause to levy for can be good outlets.
- Cut down on smoking and drinking. While alcohol and tobacco have had a character for helping you relax, they actually can make you more anxious.
- Eat well. A balanced diet can help keep your body

healthy and more suitable to handle stress. Dark chocolate and foods rich in vitamin C, like oranges and grapefruits, may lower stress hormones.

- Sculpt out some "me time" and get a little exercise. A 15 to 20 nanoseconds walk three times a week can break up your day and help you shake off stress. Contemplation, deep breathing, guided imagery or other relaxation ways can help quiet your mind.

- Get a good night's sleep. You may need to cut down on caffeine during the day and screen time at night. And a to- do list can set up the coming day and help you get a further peaceful night's sleep.

- Talk with your croaker about seeing a specialist, If these ways do n't help you manage your stress.

Stress is any change in the terrain that requires your body to reply and acclimate in response. The body reacts to these changes with physical, internal, and emotional responses. It is a normal part of life. numerous events that are to you and around you and numerous effects that you do yourself put stress on your body. You can witness good or bad forms of stress from your terrain, your body, and your studies.

Chapter 2

How Does Stress Affect Health?

The mortal body is designed to witness stress and reply to it. Stress can be positive ("eustress") similar to getting a job or being given lesser liabilities keeping us alert and ready to avoid peril. Stress becomes negative ("torture") when a person faces nonstop challenges without relief or relaxation between challenges. As a result, the person becomes trespassed and stress- related pressure builds.

Torture can lead to physical symptoms including headaches, worried stomach, elevated blood pressure, casket pain, and problems sleeping. Research suggests that stress also can bring on or worsen certain symptoms or conditions.

Stress also becomes dangerous when people use alcohol, tobacco, or medicines to try to relieve their stress. Unfortunately, rather than relieving the stress and returning the body to a relaxed state, these substances tend to keep the body in a stressed-out state and cause further problems. Consider the following;

- Forty- three percent of all grown-ups suffer adverse health goods from stress.
- Seventy- five percent to 90 of all croaker's office visits are for stress- related affections and complaints.

- Stress can play a part in problems similar to headaches, high blood pressure, heart problems, diabetes, skin conditions, asthma, arthritis, depression, and anxiety.
- The Occupational Safety and Health Administration(OSHA) declared stress a hazard of the plant. Stress costs American aid further than$ 300 billion annually.
- The continuance frequency of an emotional complaint is further than 50, frequently due to habitual, undressed stress responses.

Breathing ways for Stress Relief

- Breathing Exercises
- Aromatherapy
- Stress Reduction roster
- Take a deep breath in. Now let it out. You may notice a difference in how

you feel formerly. Your breath is an important tool to ease stress and make you feel less anxious. Some simple breathing exercises can make a big difference if you make them part of your regular routine.

Before you get started, keep these tips in mind

- Choose a place to do your breathing exercise. It could be in your bed, on your living room bottom, or in a comfortable president.
- Do not force it. This can make you feel more stressed-out.
- Try to do it at the same time formally or doubly a day.
- Wear comfortable clothes.
- Numerous breathing exercises take only a few twinkles. When you have

further time, you can do them for 10 twinkles or further to get indeed lesser benefits.

Deep Breathing

The utmost people take short, shallow breaths into their casket. It can make you feel anxious and zap your energy. With this fashion, you will learn how to take bigger breaths, all the way into your belly.

- Get comfortable. You can lie on your back in bed or on the bottom with a pillow under your head and knees. Or you can sit in a president with your shoulders, head, and neck supported against the reverse of the president.
- Breathe in through your nose. Let your belly fill with air.
- Breathe out through your nose.

- Place one hand on your belly. Place the other hand on your casket.
- As you breathe by, feel your belly rise. As you breathe out, feel your belly lower. The hand on your belly should move more than the bone that is on your casket.
- Take three further full, deep breaths. Breathe completely into your belly as it rises and falls with your breath.

Breath Focus

While you do deep breathing, use a picture in your mind and a word or expression to help you feel more relaxed.

- Close your eyes if they are open.
- Take many big, deep breaths.
- Breathe in. As you do that, imagine that the air is filled with a sense of peace

and calm. Try to feel it throughout your body.

- Breathe out. While you are doing it, imagine that the air leaves with your stress and pressure.
- Now use a word or expression with your breath. As you breathe by, say in your mind," I breathe in peace and calm."
- As you breathe out, say in your mind," I breathe out stress and pressure."
- Continue for 10 to 20 twinkles.
- Equal Time for Breathing in and Breathing Out

In this exercise, you will match how long you breathe by with how long you breathe out. Over time, you will increase how long you are suitable to breathe by and out at a time.

- Sit comfortably on the bottom or in a chair.
- Breathe in through your nose. As you do it, count to five.

- Breathe out through your nose to the count of five.
- Reprise several times.

Once you feel comfortable with breaths that last five counts, increase how long you breathe by and breathe out. You can work up to breaths that last up to 10 counts.

Progressive Muscle Relaxation

In this fashion, you breathe by as you tense a muscle group and breathe out as you release it. Progressive muscle relaxation helps you relax physically and mentally.

- Taradiddle comfortably on the bottom.
- Take many deep breaths to relax.
- Breathe in. Tense the muscles of your bases.
- Breathe out. Release the pressure in your bases.

- Breathe in. Tense your shin muscles.
- Breathe out. Release the pressure in your pins.
- Work your way up your body. Tense each muscle group. This includes your legs, belly, casket, fritters, arms, shoulders, neck, and face.
- Modified Lion's Breath

As you do this exercise, imagine that you are a captain. Let all of your breath out with a big, open mouth.

- Sit comfortably on the bottom or in a chair.
- Breathe in through your nose. Fill your belly all the way up with air.
- When you can not breathe in any more, open your mouth as wide as you can.
- Breathe out with a "HA" sound.
- Reprise several times.

Stress is normal and everyone gets it in response to situations considered hanging or dangerous. When you are stressed, your body responds by producing physical and internal responses. These stress responses can be positive, keeping you alert to peril, motivated, or adaptable to new situations.

Stress in itself isn't an illness but when you witness it constantly, it increases the threat of internal health conditions similar to depression, anxiety, psychosis, and substance use problems.

Chapter 3

Impact of Stress on Your Mental Health

Stress causes changes in the body that can range from mild to severe. Symptoms can be cognitive, physical, emotional, or behavioral. When under stress, your body's autonomic nervous system takes control. This system regulates the function of your internal organs, similar to the heart, stomach, and bowel.

Your muscles tense, there's an increase in heart rate and breathing, short-term memory becomes further effective and prepares the body for 'fight or flight' when you smell peril. Stress intensity or frequency can be good or bad. In small boluses, it can ameliorate thinking chops and help you manage in situations where you need to perform, like during a test. It can also ameliorate your capability to suppose on your bases, like figuring out a way to break a problem on the spot.

Long-term stress has signs and symptoms that you can identify to help you manage it. Some common bones include;

- Feeling overwhelmed
- Anxiety and restlessness
- Feeling hopeless and depressed
- Fear attacks
- Lack in tone-confidence

- Unfit to make opinions
- Uncaring station towards family and liabilities
- Mood swings
- Loss of appetite and trouble sleeping
- Change in sexual drive
- Unmotivated and unfocused
- Social pullout
- Drinking too important
- Reduced situations of performance and productivity

When there's stress, you're bound to witness the following;

- There is pressure or a trouble to your well-being with little or no coffers to fight the problem
- You have no network of support system in place
- You witness major life changes similar as losing a job or a change of terrain
- You are unfit to sleep at night
- You are in poor physical health
- You find it delicate to control your feelings

Manage and prioritize tasks to avoid feeling stressed-out, consider establishing a system where you address the most important tasks first and gradually work your way through the bones of lower significance.

Know your triggers Identify the types of situations that make you feel out of control, these are your triggers. When you know what your triggers are, you can avoid these situations or manage them better.

How Long Does Stress Last?

It's normal to feel stressed-out occasionally, and it can be over the short- or long- term. Long-term stress may beget unhealthy geste.

Try to help stress by avoiding your triggers and seek medical attention when you;

- Can't manage with the pressure and demands of your life
- Have studies of hurting yourself
- Have taken way to manage your stress but your symptoms persist
- Feel casket pain and experience briefness of breath, back pain, pain burning into your shoulders and arms, dizziness, or squeamish.

Numerous of us are facing challenges that can be stressful, inviting, and beget strong feelings in grown-ups and children. Public health conduct, similar to physical distancing, can make us feel isolated and lonely and can increase stress and anxiety.

After a traumatic event, people may have strong and moping responses. Learning healthy ways to manage and getting the right care and support can help reduce stressful passions and symptoms.

The symptoms may be physical or emotional. Common responses to a stressful event can include;

- Unbelief Passions of fear, shock, wrathfulness, sadness, solicitude, impassiveness, or frustration
- Changes in appetite, energy, solicitations, and interests
- Difficulty sleeping or agonies, concentrating, and making opinions
- Physical responses, similar as headaches, body pains, stomach problems, and skin rashes
- Worsening of habitual health problems
- Worsening of internal health conditions
- Increased use of tobacco, alcohol, and other substances
- It's natural to feel stress, anxiety, grief, and worry during traumatic events similar to mass blowups, natural disasters, or afflictions. Below are

ways that you can help yourself, others, and your community manage stress.

Healthy Ways to manage with Stress

Feeling emotional and nervous or having trouble sleeping and eating can all be normal responses to stress. Then there are some healthy ways you can deal with stress.

- Take breaks from watching, reading, or harkening to news stories, including those on social media. It's good to be informed but hearing about the traumatic event constantly can be disturbing. Consider limiting news to just a couple of times a day and decoupling from phone, television, and computer defenses for a while.

- Take care of yourself. Eat healthy, exercise, get plenty of sleep, and give yourself a break if you feel stressed out.
- Take care of your body.
- Take deep breaths, stretch, or meditate.
- Try to eat healthy, well-balanced reflections.
- Exercise regularly.
- Get plenty of sleep.
- Avoid inordinate alcohol, tobacco, and substance use.
- Continue with routine preventative measures(similar as vaccinations, cancer wireworks,etc.) as recommended by your healthcare provider.
- Make time to decompress. Try to do some other conditioning you enjoy.
- Talk to others. Talk with people you trust about your enterprises and how you're feeling. Partake your problems and how you're feeling and managing with a parent,

friend, counselor, croaker, or pastor.

- Connect with your community- or faith-grounded associations.
- Avoid medicines and alcohol. These may feel to help, but they can produce fresh problems and increase the stress you're formerly feeling.
- Fete when you need furtherhelp.However, talk to a psychologist, social worker, If problems continue or you're allowing about self-murder.

Chapter 4

Balancing Healthy Diet

It's easy to feel bombarded by the rearmost healthy eating trend or buzzworthy component. But good nutrition is really about constantly choosing healthy foods and potables. With healthy eating patterns, it's possible to enjoy food and potables that reflect your preferences, artistic traditions, and popular considerations.

Healthy eating emphasizes fruits, vegetables, whole grains, dairy, and protein. Dairy recommendations include low-fat or fat-free milk, lactose-free milk, and fortified soy potables. Other factory-grounded potables don't have the same nutritive parcels as beast's milk and soy potables. Protein recommendations include seafood, spare flesh and flesh, eggs, legumes (sap, peas, and lentils), soy products, nuts, and seeds.

The utmost people in the United States need to acclimate their eating patterns to increase their input of salutary fiber, calcium, vitamin D, and potassium, according to the Dietary Guidelines for Americans. At the same time, we need to consume lower added sugar, impregnated fat, and sodium. Then there are some ways to get started.

Bump Up Fiber

A mother feeding a carrot to her child

Fiber helps maintain digestive health and helps us feel fuller longer. Fiber also helps control blood sugar and lowers cholesterol situations. Fresh fruits and vegetables, whole grains, legumes, nuts, and seeds are good sources of fiber.

To impinge up fiber, try this

- Slice up raw vegetables to use as quick snacks. Storing celery and carrots in water in the refrigerator will keep them crisp longer.
- Start your day off with a whole grain cereal like oatmeal or food made with bulgur or teff. For indeed

further fiber, eclipse your cereal with berries, pumpkin seeds, or almonds.

Add half a mug of sap or lentils to your salad to add fiber, texture, and flavor.

Enjoy whole fruit, perhaps a pear, apple, melon slice or passion fruit with a mess or as cate.

Increase Calcium and Vitamin D

Calcium and vitamin D work together to promote optimal bone health. Our bodies can make vitamin D from the sun, but some individuals may have difficulty producing enough vitamin D, and too important sun exposure can increase the threat of skin cancer. While many foods naturally contain vitamin D, several foods and potables are fortified with this essential nutrient. See food sources of calcium and vitaminD.

To increase calcium and vitamin D input, try this;

- Drink a fortified dairy libation with your reflections.
- When you pack your lunch, include a packet of salmon or can of sardines once a week. Salmon and sardines with bones has further calcium than salmon and sardines without bones.
- Include spinach, collard flora, bok choy, mushrooms, and taro root in your vegetable dishes.
- Look for foods that are fortified with calcium and vitaminD. Soy potables, soy yogurt, orange juice, and some whole- grain cereals may have these added nutrients. Just be sure they don't include added sugars!

Add further Potassium

Potassium helps the feathers, heart, muscles and jitters serve duly. Not getting enough potassium can increase blood pressure, deplete calcium in bones, and increase the threat of order monuments.

People with habitual order complaints and people taking certain specifics may have too important potassium in their blood. But most people in the United States need further potassium in their eating patterns. See food sources of potassium.

To add further potassium, try this
- Try new fashions that use beet flora, lima sap, or Swiss chard.
- Put some variety in your potables with one mug of 100 pear juice or 100 pomegranate juice.
- Have a banana as a snack.
- Enjoy 100 orange juice or a recommended dairy

product with your reflections.

Limit Added Sugars

A ewer of water with bomb
Too important added sugar in your diet can contribute to weight gain, rotundity, type 2 diabetes, and heart complaint. Some foods similar to fruit and milk contain natural sugars. Added sugars are sugars and bathos that are added to foods and drinks when they're reused or prepared. Added sugars have numerous different names, similar as club juice, sludge saccharinity, dextrose, and fructose.
Table sugar, maple saccharinity, and honey are also considered added sugars. sticky drinks are a common source of added sugars.

To limit added sugars, try this
- Drink water rather than sticky drinks. Add berries or slices of lime, bomb, or

cucumber for further flavor.

- Add fruit to your cereal or yogurt for agreeableness.
- Do n't stock up on sticky drinks and snacks. rather, drink water and keep fruit and vegetable slices handy for snacks.
- At coffee shops, skip the seasoned bathos and whipped cream. Ask for low-fat or fat-free milk or a thin, fortified soy libation. Or get back to basics with black coffee.
- Read nutrition markers and choose foods with no or lower quantities of added sugars.

Replace Saturated Fats

Avocado smoothie
Replacing impregnated fat with healthier unsaturated fats can help cover your heart. Common sources of impregnated fat are adipose flesh similar to beef caricatures and link, whole milk,

full-fat rubbish, adulation, and cream rubbish.

We need some salutary fat to give us energy, help us develop healthy cells, and help us absorb some vitamins and minerals. But unsaturated fat is better for us than impregnated fat. See common sources of impregnated and unsaturated fat.

To replace impregnated fats with unsaturated fats, try this

- Replace whole milk in a smoothie with low-fat yogurt and an avocado.
- Sprinkle nuts or seeds on salads rather than rubbish.
- Use sap or seafood rather than flesh as a source of protein.
- Cook with canola, sludge, olive, peanut, safflower, soybean, or sunflower oil painting rather than adulation or margarine.
- Replace full- fat milk and rubbish with low- fat or fat-free performances.

Cut Back on Sodium

Eating too much sodium can raise your threat of high blood pressure, heart attack, and stroke. further than 70 of the sodium Americans consume comes from packaged and prepared foods. While sodium has numerous forms, 90% of the sodium we consume is from swabs. See the top sources of sodium.

To cut back on sodium, try this

- Rather of using swab, add flavor to your refections with a squeeze of bomb juice, a gusto of no- swab spice composites, or fresh sauces.
- Eat high- sodium reused and prepackaged food less constantly. numerous common foods, including viands, pizza, and deli flesh, have high quantities of sodium.
- At the grocery store, read the Nutrition Data marker to find low- sodium products.

- Buy undressed food, similar as fresh or frozen vegetables, to prepare at home without swab.

Aim for a Variety of Colors

A various mess with a variety of vegetables
A good practice is to aim for a variety of colors on your plate. Fruits and vegetables like dark, lush flora, oranges, and tomatoes indeed fresh sauces are loaded with vitamins, fiber, and minerals.

Try this
- Sprinkle fresh sauces over a salad or whole wheat pasta.
- Make a red sauce with fresh tomatoes(or canned tomatoes with low sodium or no swab added), fresh sauces, and spices.
- Add minced veggies, like peppers, broccoli, or onions to stews and omelets to give them a

boost of color and nutrients.

- Top low-fat, thin yogurt with your favorite fruit.

Manage your Stress

Nearly everyone gets stressed once in a while. Do you fete the feeling that further is anticipated of you than you can achieve? Whether at work, at home or, for illustration, on social media. Children and family can be a lot of stress, but there can also be patient pressures at work or in your free time. perhaps you're sick or you have a loved bone who's sick. You may be floundering with a relationship that isn't going well. Or perhaps fiscal problems are keeping you awake or living in a terrain of war or violence. There are so numerous circumstances that can beget pressure in our body.

Physical and internal problems

Everyone goes through stressfulperiods.However, also there isn't anything important to worry about, If you can calm down later. But if you live too long under stress and get too little rest, your body will protest. You get complaints similar to headaches, muscle pain and sleeping problems. You come perverse and still feel tired when you get out of bed. You may also feel caliginous or sad. You can come unkind to other people and you may also withdraw because contact with other people costs you too important energy. Your work takes further trouble and it's frequently delicate to concentrate. occasionally life just doesn't feel so nice presently and the prospect of enhancement seems far down.

Not everyone is inversely sensitive to stress. Especially if you want to do effects right and pay little attention to the effects that are formerly going well, you're more likely to come stressed-out.

Doing further than you can actually handle will ultimately make you less effective. exploration shows that people who work numerous hours under pressure, end up getting lower work done per hour. It can also lead to passions of depression and anxiety as well.

Chapter 5

What can you do against stress?

Relaxation against stress

Relaxation is important when you witness too much stress. Try to set away further time for yourself. Indeed if that occasionally seems insolvable. But flash back that you're less effective, and thus end up getting lower done when you're stressed. Sitting on the settee and scrolling through your phone or watching television isn't the stylish form of relaxation. Movement is better for reducing your stress. Go for a walk or exercise and try to enjoy your surroundings.

Focus on what's important to you

Say "no" more frequently to other people who want a commodity from you. Try to make a list for yourself of people and tasks that are really important to you and of effects that may not be so important at the moment. Try looking at the effects you do as a stranger. How would you look back on this 10 times? How would a close friend look at it?

Try to give your time and attention to the people and tasks that are really important to you. Make a conscious decision not to do effects that aren't important. And to spend less time with people who aren't that important to you. occasionally that can feel like losing face or giving you an anxious feeling that you aren't in control. But if you're clear to others, it can also be affable for them. fastening further on the important effects will have a positive impact on your relationship with those people who are really important in your life.

Let go of the less important effects

It can help you to leave certain tasks to someone differently. occasionally that gives the feeling that you'll lose control. That affects do n't get done the way you want them to. But if you try to do further than you can actually handle, you'll have to learn to let effects go. So you'll have to ask other people for help. This can be delicate at times, but you still need to take bold way to overcome your pride and fear of letting go.

Talk to others about your stress

It can help to open your heart to your mate or a good friend. It gives relief to look together at what's really important and what's not. And perhaps your mate has veritably different prospects of you than you always allowed.

It can also help to partake the enterprises you have. You frequently come up with much better results together or the other person would like to help you break a problem together.

To get further exercise, you can join a sports club. Go to a masseur if you regularly have muscle pain. However, you can also visit a croaker or psychologist, If all this doesn't help enough.

Also set aside time to do effects you enjoy. For illustration, a hobbyhorse, reading a book or anything else that gives you energy.

Watch what you eat. When you're stressed, you snappily turn to unhealthy food with a lot of sugars that give you some energy temporarily. But in the long run it just makes you breathless and fat. Try to eat more vegetables and fruits. You know that restless feeling when you drink too important coffee? That greatly increases your stress.

CONCLUSION

Yet, it's a commemorative for you to take into consideration these 10 ways to manage stress into productivity.

1. Exercise
2. Relax Your Muscles
3. Deep Breathing

4. Eat Well
5. Slow Down
6. Take a Break
7. Make Time for pursuits
8. Talk About Your Problems
9. Go Easy On Yourself
10. exclude Your Alarms

These days it's hard not to get overwhelmed formally once in a while. Between juggling work, family, and other commitments, you can come too stressed out and busy. But you need to set time out to de-stress or your psychological and physical health can suffer. Learning how to manage your stress takes practice, but you can, and need to do it.

Working out regularly is one of the elegant ways to relax your body and mind. Plus, exercise will ameliorate your mood. But you have to do it frequently for it to pay off.

So how important should you exercise every week?

Work up to 2 hours and 30 twinkles of relatively deep exercise like brisk walks or 75 instants of a further vigorous exercise like swimming stages, jogging or other sports. Focus on setting fitness ambitions you can meet so you don't give up. utmost flashback that doing any exercise is better than none at all.

When you're stressed, your muscles get tense. You can help loosen them up on your own and refresh your body by

- Stretching
- Enjoying a massage
- Taking a hot bath or shower
- Getting a good night's sleep

Stopping and taking many deep breaths can take the pressure off you right down. You'll be surprised how much better you feel once you get good at it. Just follow these 5 ways.

- Sit in a comfortable position with your hands in your stage and your bases on the bottom. Or you can lie down.
- Close your eyes.

- Imagine yourself in a comforting place. It can be on the sand, in a beautiful field of lawn, or anywhere that gives you a peaceful feeling.
- Sluggishly take deep breaths in and out.
- Do this for 5 to 10 twinkles at a time.

Eating a regular, well balanced diet will help you feel more in general. It may also help control your moods. Your reflections should be full of vegetables, fruit, whole grains, and spare protein for energy. And don't skip any. It's not good for you and can put you in a bad mood, which can actually increase your stress. Ultra Modern life is so busy, and occasionally we just need to decelerate down and chill out. Look at your life and find small ways you can do that. For illustration

Set your watch 5 to 10 twinkles ahead. That way you 'll get places a little early and avoid the stress of being late.

When you're driving on the track, switch to the slow lane so you can avoid road rage.

Break down big jobs into lower bones.

For illustration, don't try to answer all 100 emails if you don't have to just answer many of them.

You need to plan on some real time-out to give your mind time out from stress. However, this may be hard for you at first, If you 're a person who likes to set pretensions. But stick with it and you'll look forward to these moments. peaceful effects you can do include

- Contemplation
- Yoga
- Tai ki
- Prayer
- Harkening to your favorite music
- Spending time in nature

You need to set aside time for effects you enjoy. Try to do a commodity every day that makes you feel good, and it'll help relieve your stress. It does n't have to be a ton of time, indeed

15 to 20 twinkles will do. Relaxing pursuits include effects like

- Reading
- Knitting
- Doing an art design
- Playing golf
- Watching a movie
- Doing mystifications
- Playing cards and board games

Still, talking about them can help lower your stress, If effects are bothering you. You can talk to family members, musketeers, a trusted clergyman, your croaker, or a therapist.

And you can also talk to yourself. It's called tone- talk and we all do it. But in order for tone- talk to help reduce stress you need to make sure it's positive and not negative.

So hear nearly what you're allowing or saying when you're stressed-out. However, change it to a positive one, If you're giving yourself negative communication. For illustration, don't tell yourself "I can't do this." Tell yourself rather "I can do this," or "I'm doing this."

Accept that you can't do effects impeccably no matter how hard you try. You also can't control everything in your life. So do yourself a favor and stop allowing you to do so much. And do n't forget to keep up your sense of humor. Horselaugh goes a long way towards making you feel relaxed.

Figure out what are the biggest causes of stress in your life. Is it your job, your commute, your practice ? If you're suitable to identify what they are, see if you 're suitable to exclude them from your life, or at least reduce them.

Still, try keeping a stress journal, If you can't identify the main causes of your stress. Make note of when you come most anxious and see if you can determine a pattern, also find ways to remove or lessen those triggers.